DALE IDIENS

COOK ISLANDS ART

SHIRE ETHNOGRAPHY

2

Cover photograph
Fisherman's god; hardwood; Rarotonga.
Such figures are believed to have been intended to bring good luck to fishermen.
The inturned feet may be designed to fit into the pointed bows of a fishing
canoe. Height: 410 mm.
(Photograph: National Museums of Scotland, Ken Smith.)

British Library Cataloguing in Publication Data:
Idiens, Dale
Cook Islands art. — (Shire ethnography; 18).
1. Polynesian primitive visual arts
I. Title
709. 0110996
ISBN 0-7478-0061-8

Published by
SHIRE PUBLICATIONS LTD
Cromwell House, Church Street, Princes Risborough,
Buckinghamshire HP17 9AJ, UK.

ISBN 0 7478 0061 8

First published 1990.

Printed in Great Britain by
C. I. Thomas and Sons (Haverfordwest) Ltd,
Press Buildings, Merlins Bridge, Haverfordwest, Dyfed.

Contents

Acknowledgements

The author gratefully acknowledges the advice and assistance of George Ortiz, Geneva; John Malden, Paisley Museum and Art Galleries; Don Melvin, Island Craft Limited, Rarotonga; Dr Euan MacKie, Hunterian Museum, University of Glasgow; John McNeill, Regius Keeper, Royal Botanic Garden, Edinburgh; and Dorota Starzecka, Museum of Mankind, London.

4

List of illustrations

1
Introduction

The Pacific is the largest ocean in the world, covering almost 164 million square km (63 million square miles), over one-third of the total surface area of the planet. Apart from Papua New Guinea and New Zealand in the south-west no major land masses interrupt this immense expanse of water, and only a scattering of tiny jewel-like islands stud the vast ocean.

The islands of the Pacific are conventionally divided into three main geographical areas: Micronesia, meaning 'tiny islands'; Melanesia, or 'black islands' (a reference to the very dark-skinned populations of Papua New Guinea and adjacent groups); and Polynesia, or 'many islands'. Polynesia is the largest area and includes the Hawaiian Islands, Easter Island, New Zealand and many of the island groups of the central Pacific. The Cook Islands are part of East Polynesia (figures 1a and 1b: maps).

The Polynesian peoples who inhabit these island groups exhibit considerable genetic and linguistic homogeneity. They are generally tall and well built, with light-brown skins and straight black hair, and their languages are a branch of the widespread Austronesian language family. Present evidence, derived from archaeology and linguistics, indicates that their ancestors originated in island South-east Asia, migrating into Polynesia through Micronesia and Melanesia about three to four thousand years ago. It seems likely that the Tongan Islands were the first part of Polynesia to be settled, probably before 1300 BC. Subsequent movements rapidly populated Samoa, the Marquesas and Society Islands, and eventually, by AD 1000, New Zealand. The Cook Islands were settled between about AD 500 and 1000, chiefly from the Society Islands.

These voyagers, who travelled without maps, navigating by means of the sun or stars, wind direction, birds and the swell of the sea, were the first discoverers and settlers of the previously uninhabited islands of Polynesia. Skilled seafarers and stone-users, they brought with them the basis of a distinctive lifestyle, carrying the pigs, dogs and chickens, coconut, taro, banana and breadfruit which became the staples of Polynesian culture. Although adaptations to local circumstances were developed on each island, the material culture, social organisation and belief systems of Polynesians show a broad degree of similarity.

By the time European explorers appeared in the Pacific cen-

1a. The Pacific Ocean, showing Melanesia, Micronesia and Polynesia.

turies later to claim their 'discoveries', the inhabitants of the
Cook Islands had already established a successful existence dem-
onstrating many features common to the rest of Polynesia. As a
consequence of Western influence this way of life has suffered
considerable dislocation and much of the traditional art of the
Cook Islands is now lost. The following chapters survey, on the
basis of the limited evidence left to us, the nature of Cook Islands
art at the point of European contact.

2
The Cook Islands

Geography and history

The fifteen islands comprising the Cook group are strung out over a distance of about 1600 km (1000 miles) in the middle of the south Pacific Ocean. Their closest neighbours, the Society Islands, 640 km (400 miles) away to the north-east, Niue, 930 km (580 miles) to the west, and the Austral or Tubuai Islands, less than 480 km (300 miles) to the south-east, are nearer to some islands of the Cook group than several of the individual Cook Islands are to each other.

The total land area of the Cook Islands is only 242 square km (93 square miles), considerably less than the total land area of the Isle of Wight at 382 square km (147 square miles). The islands fall into two geographical divisions: a northern and a southern group. The northern islands, Manihiki, Nassau, Pukapuka, Rakahanga, Penrhyn, Suwarrow and Palmerston, are small coral atolls. Atolls, consisting of low narrow coral strips encircling a lagoon, are formed by reefs of coral which continue to grow from sunken volcanic islands, often 1.5 km (a mile) or more below the surface of the ocean. The highest atoll in the Cook group is no more than 3 metres (10 feet) above sea-level. They have poor soil, low rainfall, and are subject to hurricane damage. The islands to the south, Rarotonga, Mangaia, Atiu, Aitutaki, Mauke, Mitiaro, Takutea and Manuae, are larger and, with the exception of Manuae, are steep and rugged. These 'high' islands are volcanic in origin and have mountainous interiors with deep valleys, and narrow flat coastal strips encircled by a coral reef. Owing to their fertile soil, higher rainfall and dense forest cover they support the greatest populations. Rarotonga, the main island of the Cook group, is 34 km (21 miles) in periphery and its central peak is almost 652 metres (2140 feet) high (figure 2).

The first European to sight these islands was the Spaniard Alvara de Mendana, in 1595. Captain James Cook, the remarkable eighteenth-century explorer and navigator who was largely responsible for mapping the Pacific, made three visits to the islands in 1773, 1774 and 1777 and named them Hervey after a Lord of the Admiralty, Captain Hervey. Curiously, Cook himself never set foot on any island in the group, and it is one of the minor ironies of history that these are the only islands in the

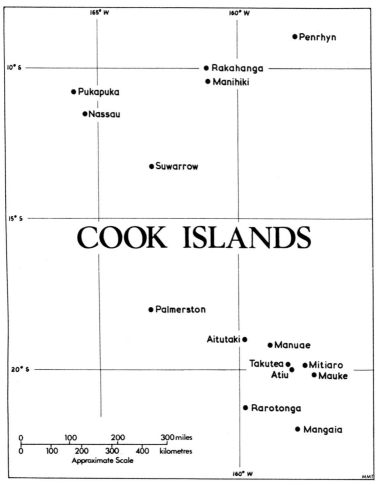

1b. The Cook Islands, Polynesia, in the south Pacific Ocean.

Pacific to bear his name. European discovery of the main island, Rarotonga, is often credited to Captain Goodenough in 1820, although sandalwood traders had preceded him six years earlier. The London Missionary Society quickly followed, setting up mission stations on Aitutaki in 1821 and Rarotonga in 1827, and the ensuing decade of intense Christian evangelism saw the rapid destruction of traditional religious forms and the decline of the old beliefs. In 1888 the Cook Islands became a British pro-

2. Te Manga, the highest peak of Rarotonga, 652 metres (2140 feet) above sea-level. (Photograph: National Museums of Scotland, Dale Idiens.)

tectorate and in 1901 were annexed to the British Empire as part of the Dominion of New Zealand. In 1965 the Cook Islands became self-governing for internal affairs, with an elected parliament advised on matters of custom by a House of Ariki (tribal chiefs). Although it is 3200 km (2000 miles) distant, the strong links with New Zealand have continued. External affairs, such as defence, are the responsibility of New Zealand. New Zealand is also the chief trading partner of the Cook Islands, and substantial numbers of Cook Islanders have emigrated to New Zealand.

Traditional life and art

The Cook Islanders have traditionally lived not in village communities but in scattered family homesteads consisting of thatched wooden houses. These are sited close to the sea or in fertile inland valleys. Although coastal dwellings are more prone to devastation by tropical hurricanes, cooling sea breezes help to keep homes comfortable in the humid climate. The islanders regarded the sea as a natural means of travel, as well as a valuable food source, and the traditional economy was a mixture of fishing and horticulture (small-scale garden agriculture). Because of the lack of large mammals on the islands (the only mammals indigenous to Polynesia are believed to be bats), fish were an important source of dietary protein. The first settlers of the Cook Islands brought with them pigs, dogs, chickens and rats, but cows and goats were introduced only by European missionaries in the nineteenth century. On the atolls of the northern Cooks there were no suitable food animals, and the basis of the economy was limited to fishing and the farming of coconut trees.

The Cook Islanders were highly skilled fishermen and used a wide variety of techniques adapted to offshore and inshore conditions. Fishing methods offshore, in the open sea beyond the reef, was an occupation for men angling with hook and line from canoes and using scoop-nets to trap flying fish. Within the reef, in the lagoon and along the shoreline, both men and women used a number of methods, working individually or in groups, groping with their hands among rocks, treading for crayfish, catching flying fish by torchlight at night, poisoning in pools, spearing, trapping, netting and angling.

The system of cultivation involved growing different plants together in small garden plots using shifting techniques. The mainstays were coconut and taro, a kind of tuber or root vegetable. Taro was grown in shallow ponds constructed in terraces between raised banks in such a way that they could be supplied by streams. Other cultivated plants included breadfruit, banana, pandanus, yam and sweet potato, and these were supplemented by the gathering of a variety of wild food products.

This way of life successfully supported sizable populations, especially on the larger islands in the southern Cooks, threatened by little except the ravages caused by an occasional hurricane or the results of warfare. On large islands such as Rarotonga, Atiu and Mangaia the population was grouped into tribal territories. At the level of the individual, life focused on the extended family system, each household consisting of a composite group of related persons who acknowledged a complex network of obligations to each other and to society as a whole. Society was structured hierarchically, authority being vested in hereditary paramount chiefs, a land-owning nobility and a priesthood. The status of each individual within this hierarchy was inherited and depended upon patrilineal (reckoned through the male line) descent being traced to a tribal ancestor. The ancestors of the most important families were regarded as deities.

This social structure was reinforced by a belief in two related

3. Arai te Tonga, an installation court with upright stone backrests for chiefs, Rarotonga. (Photograph: National Museums of Scotland, Dale Idiens.)

concepts, *mana* and *tapu*. *Mana* was the degree of power and prestige held by an individual, by his possessions and indeed by everything he touched, due to his birth and rank. *Tapu* (a word rendered in the English language as 'taboo') was a set of strict regulations designed to safeguard *mana* from pollution. Contact between persons possessing greater or lesser degrees of *mana* was restricted by the laws of *tapu* and led to elaborate regulations governing most aspects of everyday life. No one of low rank would dare to touch the person or belongings of someone with greater *mana* for fear of the consequences, which might be fatal. *Tapu* and *mana* therefore had particular significance as far as material objects were concerned.

The highest-ranking individual in any group was the senior male of the family which could trace an unbroken connection to the most important ancestor. Some ancestors achieved almost god-like status and were represented in carvings. In addition to reverence for the ancestors, Cook Islanders recognised several major deities who appear with slightly different names throughout Polynesia: Tangaroa, the creator who was also the god of the sea and fishing; Rongo, the god of peace and agriculture; and Tane, the fertility god and god of craftsmen. Many Cook Islands gods appear to have been represented by wooden carvings, often with the addition of other materials, barkcloth and coconut-fibre wrappings, feathers and shells. Religious practices invoking the ancestors centred upon open-air ceremonial areas, temples, installation courts and investiture platforms, *paepae*, for chiefs, built of stone (figures 3 and 37).

In common with their Pacific neighbours, the inhabitants of Cook Islands were stone-users, making beautifully crafted tools from stone, although shell was sometimes substituted in the northern atolls, where suitable stone was unavailable. The major resource of the Cook Islands was timber, and the Pacific hardwoods that flourished on the rich soils of the southern 'high' islands, especially *toa* (ironwood) and *tamanu* (island mahogany), were used for houses, canoes, tools, weapons, containers and ceremonial carvings. The chief form of vegetation on the northern atolls, the coconut palm, was utilised for a very wide variety of purposes.

Wood-carving was undertaken by expert male craftsmen, *ta'unga*, who were accorded special status in Cook Islands society. Other skilled crafts such as basketry, mat-making and barkcloth production were the preserve of women. The most important tool was the stone adze, the basalt head or blade secured to the wooden shaft by lashings of sennit, a cord made by plaiting or twining the fibre obtained from coconut husks. Sennit was manufactured in a variety of grades and was vital, in a culture which lacked joinery techniques and metal nails, to all forms of construction, from houses and canoes to fans and fish-hooks. A feature of woodworking technique in many cultures with a stone technology is the monoxylous, or one-piece, product. The Polynesian craftsmen in the Cook Islands had the ability to produce functional objects with elements at opposed angles and in different planes, such as four-legged stools and bowls and complex pierced and openwork decorative and ceremonial objects, without jointing separate sections together.

Wood-carving represents the peak of Cook Islands achievement in the visual arts, characterised by a sophisticated repertoire of sculptural forms, intricate engraved, painted and applied decoration, and superb finish. Many of the finest carvings, particularly renderings of the human figure, had a religious or ceremonial purpose. But surviving evidence concerning the nature and purpose of this art is limited, because missionary activity in the early nineteenth century resulted in the destruction of large numbers of Cook Islands religious carvings. A few 'idols' were rescued by the missionaries themselves and returned to England. Many of these, together with figures acquired from other Polynesian islands, were deposited in the London Missionary Society's museum as illustrations of the paganism which Christianity had overcome and are now in the collections of the British Museum. Unfortunately, few nineteenth-century missionaries appear to have been interested in recording the names of the traditional gods the different carvings represented, or which island a particular carving came from.

Since so little reliable documentation exists, scholars of Polynesian art are obliged to advance arguments for attribution on the basis of stylistic features of the carvings themselves, such as form, proportion and decoration. Sculpture from East Polynesia as a whole can be identified on the basis of common characteristics. But within this genre problems arise in differentiating between the art of groups of islands, and between the art of individual islands within each group. Unless archaeology can uncover new evidence in the future, it now seems unlikely that there will ever be certainty about the provenance of every artefact attributed to the Cook Islands.

Functional objects with no apparent religious association were not usually destroyed as a direct response to missionary zeal, although as Western culture and technology began to influence the islanders their traditional materials, methods of manufacture and artefact forms rapidly declined in use. Little of the material culture which early European visitors would have seen on the Cook Islands survives today, and it is largely to museum collections that we must turn to gain an appreciation of the range and sophistication of Cook Islands art. Those artefacts which are preserved in museums vividly demonstrate the existence before European contact of a rich artistic tradition and a remarkable level of craftsmanship in a variety of materials including stone, shell, wood, ivory, leaf, feathers and fibre.

Arguably the most important traditional artistic medium in Polynesia was oral. Societies without written records frequently develop systematic spoken traditions. In the Cook Islands, as in other parts of Polynesia, the singing and recitation of genealogy, poetry and oral history, often associated with music and dance, was of the utmost significance. These arts are now almost entirely lost.

4. Fisherman's god; hardwood painted with black designs which may relate to tattoo motifs or to patterns used for decorating barkcloth; Rarotonga. Height 315 mm. (Photograph: British Museum.)

3
Religious wood-carving

Belief in tribal gods and deified ancestors was the basis of society, and some remarkable wood-carvings from the Cook Islands are believed to represent or be associated with traditional gods such as Tangaroa, the creator and god of the sea, and Tane, the god of craftsmen. Although only a limited quantity of religious and ceremonial carvings survives, the range and variety is such that for the purposes of study they may be grouped in two categories, figurative and abstract. The problems of associating particular carvings with individual islands have already been referred to. A welcome exception in the Cook Islands is the figurative and abstract carving of Rarotonga, which is sufficiently distinctive to be unmistakable.

The wooden figure itself may have been only one element in the total configuration of a god. Many Cook Islands wood-carvings still bear the remains of additional components, such as attached sprays of feathers and fine sennit and barkcloth bindings with concealed insertions of feather tufts or discs of pearl-shell, while the pierced ears of figures sometimes supported ivory pendants. The islanders have always adorned their own bodies with scented flowers and leaves, especially on ceremonial occasions, and it is quite possible that the wooden figures of gods were 'dressed' for ritual appearances with a profusion of ephemeral accessories, iridescent, vivid and perfumed. Some of the additional materials, such as red feathers, were themselves sacred, so it was the assemblage rather than the wooden core that had the highest spiritual status. On a few islands the most important deities were represented not by carvings in wood, but by bundles of barkcloth, feathers and woven sennit alone. This tradition may relate to practice in the Society Islands, where a major Tahitian god, Oro, was represented in a cylindrical sennit form.

Other intangible but nonetheless compelling elements contributed to the sacred status and symbolism of religious objects, or, as described by one expert, they carried 'non-visual information'. To the initiated, each figure or representation reverberated with the *mana* or power of past associations with individuals, events and histories, recalled by song, recitation and chanting.

Figurative carvings

Sculptures in the form of a single figure survive from both Aitutaki and Rarotonga. The carvings from each island are distinctive in style, although the typical East Polynesian form of a frontal figure (usually, if gender is marked, male) standing upright or with the legs flexed, arms and hands generally resting on the torso, the head often of a disproportionately large size to the body, is always clear. Some scholars advocate that the enlarged head and the characteristically prominent belly and penis express values and beliefs concerning power and fertility.

The most familiar and most frequently reproduced Cook Islands form is the squat and powerful figure of the 'fisherman's god' (see cover) from Rarotonga. So-called because they are thought to have been placed in the bows of fishing canoes to provide protection from peril at sea and bring good luck to the fisherman, the feet of these figures are sometimes inclined inwards, perhaps to fit more neatly into the point of the canoe bows. The figures illustrate the symmetrical profile of jaw, arm and thigh, the elliptical definition of eye, eyelids and brow, lips and tongue, and the distinctive treatment of ear and navel which mark figure sculpture from Rarotonga. Many of these figures have had the large carved phallus cut off by European collectors.

Some fisherman's gods are painted with striking black geometric designs (figure 4). A few figure carvings from other islands in the group (figure 12) and ceremonial items such as drums are also decorated with black patterns, indicating that many Cook Islands objects may have been painted. The designs are similar to those used in tattooing the human body, a practice once widespread in the Cook Islands, and to some motifs in patterns on barkcloth. The black pigment used to paint wooden objects was probably made from the burnt kernels of candle-nuts; this was also employed in tattooing and in painting and dyeing barkcloth.

Two extraordinary figure carvings survive from Rarotonga which appear to be related since both support smaller secondary figures (figures 5 and 6). Taller than the fisherman's gods, they present the same general posture with flexed legs and arms, the latter resting on the enlarged abdomen, typical of figure sculpture from East Polynesia, although the body proportions, especially of the larger figure, are more naturalistic than usual. The prominent curved shapes of eye, eyelid and brow, and the thrust of the jaw following that of the arm and belly define the classic Rarotongan form. The superb degree of finish to the surface of the larger figure (figure 5), leaving almost no trace of tool marks,

5. (Left) Figure of a god; ironwood; Rarotonga. Secondary figures are carved on the chest and arms. The arms are also wrapped with sennit cord. The feet have been built up by a museum conservator to enable the piece to stand. Height 690 mm. (Photograph: British Museum.)

6. (Right) Figure of a god; hardwood; Rarotonga. Secondary figures are carved on the chest and buttocks. The pierced ears once supported the ivory pendants illustrated in figure 39 suspended on cords of human hair. Height 565 mm. (George Ortiz Collection. Photograph: Ken Smith.)

7. (Left) Figure of a god; hardwood; Aitutaki. Standing on a decorated base with a central support, with bands of zigzags carved across the chest, this figure is clearly part of another object, most probably a canoe. Height 406 mm. (Photograph: Hunterian Museum, University of Glasgow.)

8. (Right) Figure of a female deity; hardwood; Aitutaki. The base, decorated with incised chevrons, has a rear support. Height 525 mm. (Photograph: British Museum.)

is a feature of many religious and ceremonial carvings from Rarotonga. Even when partly unfinished, as seen in the surface of the torso and limbs of the second figure (figure 6), the dense tropical hardwood takes on a fine glossy patina over time. The reason for the unfinished state of the second figure is not known; it may have been that the lower body was intended to be concealed by a ritual wrapping of barkcloth, or that the sculptor for some reason was unable to complete his task.

The particular feature which relates these two figures is the addition of smaller figures, either in high or low relief on the body. The most clearly defined of the secondary figures have large ears, pronounced brow and nasal bridges, a well marked mouth and chin and the typical Rarotongan eye form of opposed curves. Sometimes the navel and penis are indicated, and the arms and legs are generally rudimentary. Similar features are marked to a greater or lesser degree on all the additional figures on these two sculptures, and it seems likely that on Rarotonga there was a tradition of images characterised by the proliferation and superimposition of secondary figures. A similar genre existed on Rurutu in the neighbouring Austral Islands. We do not know which gods these figures represent although among possibilities which have been suggested are Tangaroa, the Polynesian god of creation, in the process of generating other gods and men, and an ancestor deified as the founder of a lineage.

Figure carvings attributed to Aitutaki are generally less massive in style than those of Rarotonga. Their basic proportions and posture still conform to the typical East Polynesian mode (figure 7) but the limbs are more slender and attenuated and a pedestal or base with a vertical support between the legs is occasionally provided. Sometimes the treatment of the facial features is similar to that of Rarotonga, but in other examples it changes (figure 8) and seems less elaborate and assured, while geometric decoration in the form of zigzags and chevrons on the base, and occasionally on the figure itself, appears more frequently.

Abstract carvings

Much religious and ceremonial wood-carving from the Cook Islands is so highly stylised as to be abstract. In some carvings elements of the design appear to relate to the human form while in others this is less clear. Several wood-carvings known as 'staff gods' survive from Rarotonga, each consisting of a pole cut from ironwood. Some of these are over 5.5 metres (18 feet) long while the smallest example is barely 770 mm (30 inches). One or both

ends are elaborately carved while the central shaft is left plain to
support a lavish ceremonial wrapping of painted barkcloth,
which concealed red feathers and discs of pearlshell, representing the spirit of the god. In many cases this wrapping has been
lost, and sometimes the shaft has been cut down by Europeans
for ease of transport so that only the ornamented upper part
remains. Missionary documentation of these staff gods in the
early nineteenth century is unusually detailed, and there are first-
hand descriptions of the way in which they were carried upright
with the bottom edge of the barkcloth bundle supported on cross-
bars. At least fourteen staff gods were surrendered to London
Missionary Society representatives on a single occasion in 1827.

The typical 'head' section of a staff god (figure 9) shows the
same characteristic features of eye, mouth and ear as the single
figures from Rarotonga, although the form of the head itself has
narrowed to a slender wedge. Below the head a series of conjoined stylised figures alternate in frontal and profile positions.
These figures have the same large ears and eye, brow and nose
forms as the secondary figures superimposed on the two large
figure sculptures from Rarotonga (figures 5 and 6). They
reappear at the lower end of the staff god, which terminates in a
phallus (figure 9).

A unique version of a Rarotongan staff god (figure 10) is surmounted by a pair of standing figures instead of a single head.
Below the two standing figures are two rows of smaller stylised
figures and a section of plain shaft (the barkcloth wrap is missing)
above a phallic terminal. The purpose of these staff gods and the
beliefs embodied in their fascinating abstraction can only be
guessed at. It has been suggested that they are the genealogical
staves of principal family lineages on Rarotonga, or that the suc-
cession of secondary figures represents generations of ancestors
surmounted by the creator god, Tangaroa. The emphasis given to
the ears of the secondary figures has led to the theory that
Taranganui or 'Great Ears', an ancestral figure, is represented.
These same little stylised figures with large ears appear on other
objects from Rarotonga. They dance around the terminal of a
ceremonial staff (figure 11) and fringe the edges of a spectacular
canoe sternpiece (figure 27).

Further degrees of abstraction are evident in a number of carvings from the islands of Aitutaki, Mitiaro and Mangaia. A tanta-
lising carving from Aitutaki consists of a bevelled bar supporting
a pair of arching conjoined figures entirely covered with a finely
detailed geometric pattern in black paint (figure 12). The head,

9. (Left and right) Staff god; Rarotonga. Detail of the upper end (left) and the lower end (right) of a carved ironwood staff showing a stylised wedge-shaped head above secondary figures in frontal and profile positions. The plain shaft (not illustrated) between this and the lower end would once have supported a massive roll of barkcloth wrapping containing red feathers and pieces of pearlshell symbolising the essence of the god. The lower end is carved with a phallus below stylised secondary figures in frontal and profile positions. Length of upper end detail 560 mm; length of lower end 505 mm; length of entire piece 3.030 metres. (Photographs: National Museums of Scotland, Ken Smith.)

10. (Left) Staff god; ironwood; Rarotonga. A pair of figures surmounts two rows of secondary figures above a plain shaft, which would once have supported a barkcloth wrapping. Below are further secondary figures above a carved phallus. Length 820 mm. (Photograph: British Museum.)

11. (Right) Staff; Rarotonga. Detail of the upper end of an ironwood staff, the terminal carved with four secondary figures with large ears like those on the wood-carvings in figures 5, 6, 9 and 10. The purpose of this staff is not known, although it must have had some ceremonial function. Length of detail 910 mm; length of complete staff 2.480 metres. (Photograph: National Museums of Scotland, Ken Smith.)

12. Conjoined figures on a bar; wood with black painted decoration; Aitutaki. Apart from some paint loss, this object is complete. Its purpose is unknown. Length 390 mm. (Photograph: Hunterian Museum, University of Glasgow.)

torso and limbs of the two figures are stylised and the facial features indicated solely by paint. The carving is complete and, apart from some paint loss, undamaged; its meaning and purpose are unknown.

Tiny arched forms, which appear to be miniature versions of the two figures on a bar from Aitutaki, orbit the shafts of small carvings from Mitiaro (figure 13). These rare sculptures are sometimes described in the literature as 'mace gods', because they bear pierced mace-like terminals above delicate openwork shafts. The fragile arches, which may have functioned as cleats for feather tassels, are often broken and missing. The sennit, barkcloth and feather attachments which partly survive on the two examples here are also frequently lost.

Similar abstractions reverberate about the complex upper sections of a type of mace god from Mangaia (figure 14). An extraordinary array of pillars, arches and incised geometric decoration has been achieved by piercing and cutting away the wood in systematic stages so that the final result rests for effect as much on the areas of free space as on the wooden structure itself. The shaft is tightly bound with fine sennit cord securing vertical holders for feather decorations which are now lost, and the lower part of the shaft is further covered by a wrap of thick sennit cord wound with human hair. The surface decoration of the arches consists of repetitive raised geometric motifs which some scholars have styled 'K-forms'. These motifs are produced by cutting into

13. (Above) Mace gods; hardwood, with additions of sennit, barkcloth and feathers; Mitiaro. Height of the example on the right 386 mm. (Paisley Museum and Art Galleries. Photograph: Ken Smith.)

14. (Right) Mace god; hardwood decorated with carved K-forms, with additions of sennit, feathers (now lost) and human hair; Mangaia. Height 900 mm. (Photograph: British Museum.)

15. (Left) Slab god; hardwood; Aitutaki. Roughly carved with zigzag bands in relief and a pierced lozenge form. Height 310 mm. (Photograph: Hunterian Museum, University of Glasgow.)

16. (Right) Slab god; hardwood; Aitutaki. Incised with horizontal rows of triangles and lozenges between zigzag bands in relief. The lower section and the back have barkcloth wrapping secured by sennit cord and tufts of coconut fibre. Length 490 mm. (Photograph: British Museum.)

the surface of the wood to remove small triangular and rhomboidal sections, leaving portions of the original surface standing out in relief. K-forms are used widely in Cook Islands art, appearing, for example, as 'double-K' designs on slit gongs (figure 29) and adze handles (figures 34 and 35) from Mangaia. K-forms are also a feature of much decoration on wooden objects from the neighbouring Austral Islands. When used to cover large curved or flat surfaces they create an intricate faceted effect which has an almost metallic brilliance in strong light. Opinions differ as to whether K-forms derive from an ultimate abstraction of the human form or are purely geometric in inspiration.

The abstraction of Aitutaki religious carving can be extreme, extending to a number of flat wooden forms some of which are so simply essayed as to suggest a ritual 'shorthand' that could be easily understood without detailed elaboration. As a group, such wood-carvings from Aitutaki are called 'slab gods'. They are usually flat and slab-like and often decorated on both sides, with shaped spatulate handle or grip. The simplest versions (figure 15) are ornamented with zigzag bands in relief and incised or pierced triangular or lozenge shapes of the kind which appear as decoration on some Aitutaki figures (see figures 7 and 8). More elaborate slab gods from Aitutaki (figure 16) bear ornamentation suggesting rhythms which link the little secondary big-eared figures from Rarotonga, the openwork mace gods of Mitiaro, Mangaia's pierced abstractions and the two conjoined Aitutaki figures.

It is tempting to grope for the missing pieces of this puzzle and speculate on the scope and meaning of traditional Cook Islands art. The stylised staff gods of Rarotonga, the abstract shapes of Aitutaki, Mitiaro and Mangaia and the reiteration of surface K-forms may suggest relationships to the Western observer, but there are too few objects and too little information to sustain a thorough analysis. We can, however, enjoy the remarkable objects from the Cook Islands which have been preserved as a unique and important aspect of the artistic heritage of mankind.

4
Functional wood-carving

The traditional material culture of the Cook Islands included a wide range of functional wooden objects made for domestic purposes, for fishing and farming, for recreation and for war. Decoration on artefacts of everyday use was generally limited and often entirely lacking. But the design and form of utilitarian wood-carving in the Cook Islands frequently achieve a proportion and balance, a sculptural quality, that merit inclusion in a survey of art.

Cooked food was generally prepared by steaming in the earth oven (a pit in which food was placed on top of heated stones, covered with leaves and earth) and mixed and served in bowls of varying sizes. These were round or oval in shape, the latter occasionally pointed at one end to assist the pouring of liquid. Regardless of size or shape, bowls were sometimes made with four short legs carved in one with the body of the vessel. Some scholars have suggested that legless bowls may be the earlier form, those with legs postdating the introduction of metal tools, which made it easier to carve such pieces. There is no evidence either to support or to refute this theory, although a variety of traditional Cook Islands artefacts, including stools, pounding tables and coconut graters, all have legs. The capacity of craftsmen to carve very large objects may also have been enhanced by the use of metal implements and a small number of impressive oversized vessels from the Cook Islands in museum collections attest to the scale of their skill. The massive example of a canoe-shaped bowl on four legs (figure 17) which can hold 1364 litres (300 gallons) was given by Poaru, king of Atiu, to Tetuanuireiaiteraiatea, a chieftainess of Haapiti, on Eimeo Island in the Society group in 1871. The immense size of this vessel, which was carved from a single piece of *tamanu* (island mahogany), a tree grown in burial places and regarded as sacred, emphasised the status of its owner. Such containers were used at large communal feasts for the preparation of poi, a favourite Polynesian dish of fermented taro or plantain mash. The inhabitants of Atiu also produced large cylindrical legless vessels to contain a home-brewed beer which was consumed on social occasions (figure 18). The vessel, *tumunu*, was made from the hollowed-out lower section of a coconut palm, the entire tree being destroyed to obtain this section. Several *tumunus* were still in regular use in the 1980s

17. Canoe-shaped vessel on four legs; Atiu. Carved from a single piece of *tamanu* and with a capacity of 1364 litres. Used at major feasts to hold poi, a mash of taro, a root vegetable, or plantain. Length 3.660 metres. (Photograph: National Museums of Scotland.)

around the area of the main village on Atiu. Bowls of lesser girth, like the four-legged bowl from Mauke island called *Takapua,* meaning friend or neighbour (figure 19), were used by the family members of a homestead to make poi. On the northern atolls coconut shells were used for cooking and as containers, because of the lack of suitable timber. A few northern islands produced carved wooden bowls, and those of Manihiki are inlaid with pearlshell (figure 20). The Cook Islands appear not to have produced special bowls for kava, a drink made from the root of a pepper plant. The preparation and serving of this beverage had great social significance in other parts of Polynesia, such as Samoa, Tonga and Fiji. Kava was made in the Cook Islands but its use lacked the same ceremonial importance as elsewhere.

Both cooked and raw food was processed by being crushed with a heavy pounder of basalt, calcite or coral (figure 36). On the northern atolls suitable stone was not available and wooden pounders were traditionally produced. However, it appears that European collectors removed so many of the stone pounders that they too were gradually replaced by wooden examples. The pounder was used on a circular wooden pounding table (figure 21). These have a carefully shaped pointed underside to withstand the impact of pounding. Another important implement for food processing was the coconut grater, a four-legged curved wooden seat with a projecting arm supporting a blade of shell,

18. (Right) Cylindrical vessel; Atiu. Carved from the lower part of the trunk of a coconut tree and used for home-brewed beer. Collected in 1983 by Don Melvin. Height 870 mm. (Photograph: National Museums of Scotland, Ken Smith.)

19. (Below) Bowl on four legs; Mauke. Carved from a single piece of wood in a similar form to the vessel illustrated in figure 17. This bowl is called *Takapua*, meaning a friend or neighbour. Length 1.015 metres. (Photograph: National Museums of Scotland, Ken Smith.)

20. Bowl; Manihiki. Carved wood inlaid with discs of pearlshell around the rim and on one side. Pearlshell inlay is characteristic of Manihiki art. Height 246 mm. (Photograph: Hunterian Museum, University of Glasgow.)

21. Pounding table on four legs; monkey pod wood, carved in a single piece. The pointed underside strengthens the centre of the table to withstand the action of the stone pounder traditionally used to crush food. Replica of a traditional Atiu form, carved by Don Melvin and Puna Tu of Island Craft Limited, Rarotonga, in 1983. Diameter 595 mm. (Photograph: National Museums of Scotland, Ken Smith.)

coral or later iron, lashed on with sennit. The operator sat astride
this seat and scraped out the open coconut on the blade so that
the meat fell into a container below.

A most necessary item of personal domestic equipment in the
humid Pacific climate was the fan, used to keep away insects and
as a shade from the sun. Those for common use were plain with

22. Fan; plaited coconut-leaf flap and wooden handle carved with two stylised back-to-
back figures; Rarotonga. Finely made fans with carved handles like this example were
symbols of rank. The documentation associated with this fan states that it was collected
on Tahiti in the Society Islands, although the treatment of the heads of the two figures
on the handle is clearly in the classic Rarotongan style. Height 460 mm. (Photograph:
National Museums of Scotland, Ken Smith.)

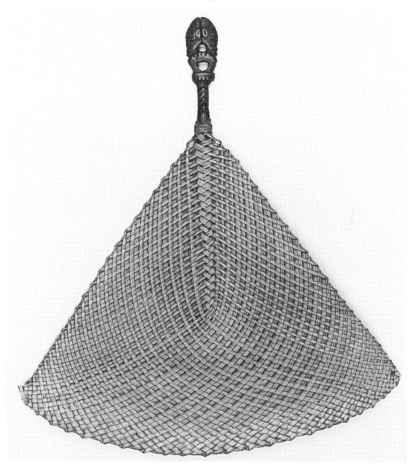

23. Stool on four legs; monkey pod wood, carved in a single piece. Traditionally only chiefs were entitled to stools, and lesser ranks sat on the floor. Replica of a traditional Atiu form, carved by Puna Tu of Island Craft Limited, Rarotonga, in 1983. Length 390 mm. (Photograph: National Museums of Scotland, Ken Smith.)

simply plaited coconut-leaf flaps and handles fashioned from the midrib of the coconut leaf itself or of plain wood. Examples with more finely worked flaps of pandanus leaf and wooden handles carved with figurative decoration belonged to individuals of high rank (figure 22) and symbolised their authority. Wooden fan handles carved with a pair of stylised back-to-back figures are a feature of the art of East Polynesia. In the Society and Austral Islands the flap of the fan becomes a whisk of coconut fibre below a pair of highly abstract compressed figures surmounting the handle. Rarotongan carved fan handles demonstrate a range of abstractions, although usually the characteristic Rarotongan eye and mouth forms and the enlarged head remain discernible.

Furniture in the Cook Islands was minimal and consisted of mats, headrests and low stools. The stools were reserved for the use of chiefs; other ranks of society sat on the floor. Stools were made on Aitutaki and Rarotonga, but the characteristic Cook Islands form derives from Atiu (figure 23). This Polynesian shape, the curve of the seat counterpointed by the curves of four legs on heart-shaped feet, originated in the Society Islands and spread to Western Tuamotu, the Austral Islands and the southern Cook group (with the exception of the island of Mangaia). On the Cook Islands these stools were traditionally carved from *tamanu*.

Houses were generally built to a rectangular plan and walled with cane or wood, the ridged roofs thatched with coconut or pandanus leaves. Ornamental sennit lashings secured the rafters to the uprights, which were sometimes set on raised platforms of stone with a stone-faced terrace or veranda in front of the building. Kitchens or cookhouses were separate structures, and houses were also built as canoe stores, shelters for barkcloth makers, and to hold religious paraphernalia in the open-air temples or *marae*.

24. Shark hook; wood, with wrapped sennit line and grooved stone sinker; Mangaia. Length of hook 275 mm. (Photograph: British Museum.)

25. Single-outrigger canoe; Atiu. Dug-out hull with separate gunwales, prow and stern pieces, seat, outrigger and outrigger arms attached with sennit lashings. A traditional one-man fishing canoe, made in 1983 by Parua Arika, Sam Koronui, Miro Tedrea and Vainepoto Nookura. Length 4.770 metres. (Photograph: National Museums of Scotland, Ken Smith.)

Farming equipment included pointed stakes for stripping off the outer fibrous husks from coconuts, long poles for pulling down fruit from high branches, and carrying poles for supporting burdens.

Barkcloth was processed with wooden beaters of the usual square-sectioned Polynesian type on wooden anvils. Wooden fish-hooks of various sizes were traditionally used, but these were rapidly replaced by European metal hooks. Large one-piece wooden hooks, sometimes decorated, for taking shark are rare survivals (figure 24).

Canoes were important for fishing, for trade and for war. These wooden vessels, the hulls hollowed out with stone adzes and the superstructure lashed or stitched with sennit cordage, were the most complex items of technology produced in the Cook Islands. One-man single-outrigger canoes for coastal fishing and transport are still being made on some islands (figure 25).

The islanders made highly sophisticated double-hulled canoes, 15 to 24 metres (50 to 80 feet) long and capable of transporting large numbers of people for great distances. With such vessels, or their prototypes, the ancestors of today's Polynesians discovered and settled the Cook Islands. No full-size examples of this type of vessel survive today. Canoe models made for sale in the nineteenth century are thought to reproduce the general principles of the originals although details may be inaccurate. Some double canoes, such as those made on Atiu, had a defined bow and stern and fixed sails and could change direction only by the inefficient method of tacking, that is steering the vessel round on a new course rather than changing ends. But on Manihiki double canoes of greater versatility (figure 26), with the bow of each dug-out hull pointing in opposite directions and a lateen sail rigged like those on a single-outrigger canoe, so that it could be swung around on the mast, were able to sail either end forward. Model canoes from Manihiki are often decorated with discs of pearlshell inlay, a characteristic feature of workmanship on this island. It is probable that the bow and stern sections of these models have been enlarged to give a greater surface area for decorative inlay.

Sternpieces decorated with carved and pierced openwork were made for some important canoes, possibly those used by chiefs in warfare. A few of these have been collected by Europeans because of their carving and are now preserved in museums (figure 27). Paddles were sometimes decorated with carving and

26. Model double-hulled canoe; wood, coconut leaf, pearlshell and sennit cord; Manihiki. The bows of each hull point in opposite directions and the lateen sails can be swung round on the masts so the vessel can quickly change direction. Length 740 mm. (Photograph: National Museums of Scotland, Ken Smith.)

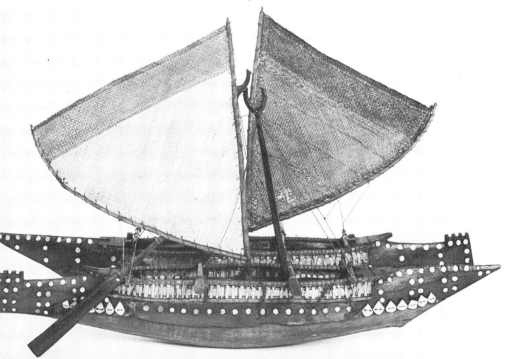

27. Canoe stern-piece; wood, the edges carved with rows of pierced stylised figures with large ears; Rarotonga. The square perforations at the base are presumed to be for sennit lashing to secure the piece to a canoe. Height 680 mm. (Photograph: British Museum.)

inlay, and different islands in the Cook group produced distinctive forms of bailer, an essential and standard item of equipment in the Polynesian outrigger canoe, which easily became swamped in high seas (figure 28).

Carved wooden drums and gongs were made for ceremonial and secular music. The upright form of drum using a hollowed section of tree-trunk and a tympanum of sharkskin did not survive long into the contact period and examples are now rare. Horizontal slit gongs, carved from a single section of tree-trunk, had no skin tympanum and resonated when struck directly by a beater. They were used for signalling, for recreation and for ceremonial occasions. The most important ceremonial gongs were elaborately decorated with carving (figure 29) and sometimes painting. Simpler versions were made for everyday secular use (figure 30), and this form has persisted into the twentieth century. A variety of games was played, using wooden devices

28. Canoe bailer, carved from a single piece of *tamanu*. An essential item of equipment for both outrigger and large canoes. Replica of a traditional Mauke form carved by Apii Tuariki of Island Craft Limited, Rarotonga, in 1983. Length 295 mm. (Photograph: National Museums of Scotland, Ken Smith.)

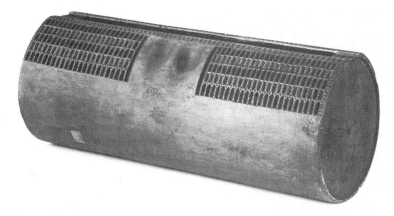

29. Ceremonial slit gong, carved in one piece from a single section of tree-trunk; Mangaia. The upper sides are incised with geometric ornaments including chevrons and K-forms. Length 910 mm. (Photograph: British Museum.)

30. Slit gong, carved from a single piece of *tamanu* (island mahogany), and beater of *toa* (ironwood); Rarotonga. This traditional form is still being made for use partly in performances designed for tourists. Carved by Puna Tu of Island Craft Limited, Rarotonga, in 1983. Length of slit gong 505 mm. (Photograph: National Museums of Scotland, Ken Smith.)

31. Game discs; hardwood. Traditional designs made at Island Craft Limited on Rarotonga in 1981 for sale as souvenirs to tourists. On the left a replica of an Atiu throwing disc (except for the pearlshell inlay which is not traditional). Diameter 130 mm. On the right a replica of a Mangaia disc for pitching. (Photograph: National Museums of Scotland, Ken Smith.)

such as tops, balls and stilts. A popular game on Mangaia involved pitching wooden discs on a plaited coconut-leaf mat, and on other islands in the group wooden discs were thrown on roads and pathways (figure 31).

Like other Polynesians, the Cook Islanders were warlike and armed conflict was frequent. Land-owning chiefs fought to expand their territories, family feuds were perpetuated by revenge taking and rivalry between tribal groups quickly became outright hostility. The larger southern islands produced a variety of wooden clubs and spears. The typical Rarotongan form was a long pole-club (figure 32) with curving serrated edges to the head or blade, described by Captain Cook as 'nicely scalloped'. This is one of the most beautiful and sophisticated styles of Pacific weapon, made from *toa* (ironwood). The curved designs edging the blades of these clubs are very varied, and occasionally tiny stylised figures emerge from the surface. Decorative bands encircle the shaft below the blade and often the butt is given a phallic shape. It seems likely that this was intended to emphasise the power and aggressiveness needed by the warrior in warfare. Clubs of shorter length were produced, for example on Mangaia. Hardwood spears with wooden points, sometimes carved with double pairs of barbs, were also part of the armoury.

All Cook Islands wood-carving was the work of specialist male

32. Pole-clubs; iron-wood; Rarotonga. Detail of the heads only, to show the variety of design. The example on the left is unusual in having three tiny stylised human figures carved on the centre of the blade on both sides. Length of detail shown of club on left 1.095 metres; length of entire club 2.250 metres. (Photograph: National Museums of Scotland, Ken Smith.)

33. Adze; the basalt head lashed with braided sennit to a plain wood shaft; Mangaia. The adze was the primary traditional working tool of the Cook Islands, replaced rapidly by metal implements after contact with Europeans in the late eighteenth century. Length 640 mm. (Photograph: National Museums of Scotland, Ken Smith.)

craftsmen. Their principal tool was a basalt adze-head lashed with sennit to a plain wooden handle (figure 33). On Mangaia ceremonial adzes believed to symbolise Tane, the god of carpentry, were traditionally produced with no apparent functional purpose (figure 34). The basalt blade was joined to the shaft with decorative sennit lashing of great fineness, and the handles were decorated with double K motifs, a repeated pattern which may represent stylised human figures. Ceremonial adzes continued to

Cook Islands Art

34. Ceremonial adze; the basalt head lashed with sennit to a straight wooden shaft ornamented with carved K-forms; Mangaia. This is the traditional form of ceremonial adze before the form began to become elaborated for sale to Europeans. Length 670 mm. (Photograph: National Museums of Scotland, Ken Smith.)

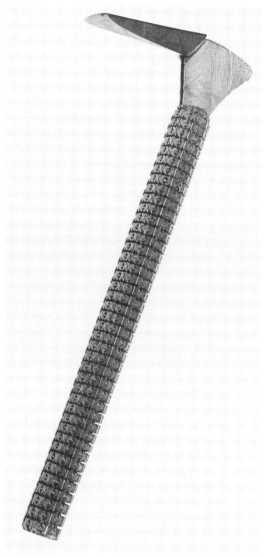

be made in the nineteenth century to satisfy the European souvenir trade, and increasingly large and elaborate handles of pierced and stepped pedestal form became fashionable to meet this demand (figure 35).

5
Other materials

Stone technology was a fundamental part of traditional Cook Islands culture. Deposits of basalt on the southern volcanic islands in the group provided a dense hard stone. When worked by the only means available, laboriously flaking and grinding with other stones, polishing with coral and a species of seaweed and water, basalt could be transformed into the cutting and pounding implements needed to shape all the material essentials of life, houses, canoes, tools and weapons.

Chisels, scrapers and pounders were made from stone, but the most important tool was the adze. The refinement of the Polynesian hardstone adze-head developed over a very long period, and the small variations in adze design serve to differentiate island groups and even individual islands. The adze-head is bevelled at one end to give a cutting edge and the other tanged end is secured with sennit lashing to the wooden shaft in such a way that the planes of shaft and edge are at right angles. This feature distinguishes the adze from the axe, where the cutting edge and shaft are in the same plane. In Polynesia the axe was not known and the adze appears to have been used almost exclusively. As mentioned earlier, the use of sennit as a fastening was of enormous importance. The twining and plaiting of fibre from the husks of coconuts to produce sennit was a distinctive art in Polynesia and in some groups was regarded as an appropriate activity even for chiefs. Suitable fibre was obtainable only from particular varieties of coconut and the process of manufacture was laborious and complex. The functional basis of sennit fastening was often transformed, for example in house construction and on ceremonial adzes (figure 35), into complex decoration by means of cleverly wrapping and layering the cord. Besides being used as a means of fastening, sennit was important as cordage, for fishing lines and nets, and was also used for articles of dress, such as the conical hats worn by warriors on Atiu.

Heavy pounders were needed to process certain foods, particularly root vegetables such as taro, which was a staple of Cook Islands diet. Food pounders were made from basalt, but on islands where suitable stone was unavailable other materials such as coral were used, and on Mangaia deep caves provided calcite deposits for this purpose (figure 36). Shaped stones were used as

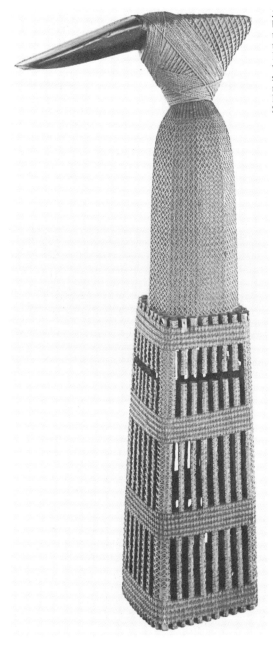

35. Ceremonial adze; the basalt head lashed with sennit to an elaborate pierced pedestal decorated with K-forms; Mangaia. Adzes of this type were made for the Western souvenir trade. Height 630 mm. (Photograph: National Museums of Scotland, Ken Smith.)

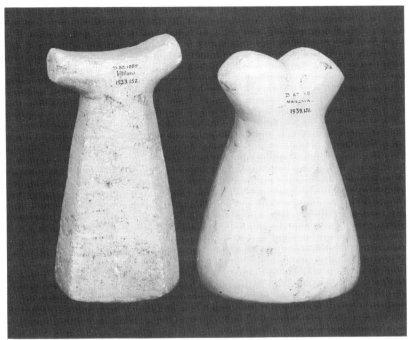

36. Food pounders; calcite; the example on the left from Mitiaro, that on the right from Mangaia. Used to process food on wooden pounding tables (see figure 21). Height of the example on the left 155 mm. (Photograph: National Museums of Scotland, Ken Smith.)

missiles in warfare, and also as sinkers for fishing nets and hooks (figure 24).

The durability of stone was exploited for building the foundation platforms of wooden domestic houses and the veranda-style terraces fronting them, and also in the construction of permanent ceremonial centres. Along the coastal area of Rarotonga a great processional way, partially paved with natural basalt blocks, encircled the island. Accessible from this road were a number of open-air religious and ceremonial structures built of stone. Some were temple enclosures, or *marae*, having a basic plan of a rectangular court, often paved and walled, with a stone platform running across one end to support a wooden godhouse to hold religious paraphernalia. Others were courts for the investiture and installation of chiefs of different ranks (figure 3) or platforms for the same purpose (figure 37) with pavements of natural basalt boulders and stone seats with upright backrests for chiefs. Stone images representing traditional gods were once a feature of the

37. *Paepae* Temaru-o-te-ta'iti, Rarotonga. T-shaped investiture platform paved with natural basalt boulders, shown looking from the platform area down the approach path. A stone backrest is visible on the right. Originally the surface of the path and platform would have been flat. (Photograph: National Museums of Scotland, Dale Idiens.)

marae, but these were all defaced and destroyed in the early nineteenth century by Christian converts. The special godhouses on the *marae*, together with the religious wood-carvings which were stored in them are also lost, but a number of the stone platforms remain and several of these have been excavated.

The use of ornament to signal rank or affiliation, or purely for love of display, exploited a wide range of materials. Permanent body decoration in the form of tattooing (the English term 'tattoo' derives from the Polynesian word *tatau*) was a mark of status for both men and women. The tip of a notched bone comb tied to a wooden handle was dipped in a black pigment made from burnt candle-nuts and the comb was then tapped with a small beater to pierce the skin. Designs were usually geometric. The arms and legs only might be patterned, or on occasion the entire body.

Breast ornaments of silvery cut and polished pearlshell were worn throughout the Cook group (figure 38), especially by warriors and important individuals. Highly prized cetacean ivory,

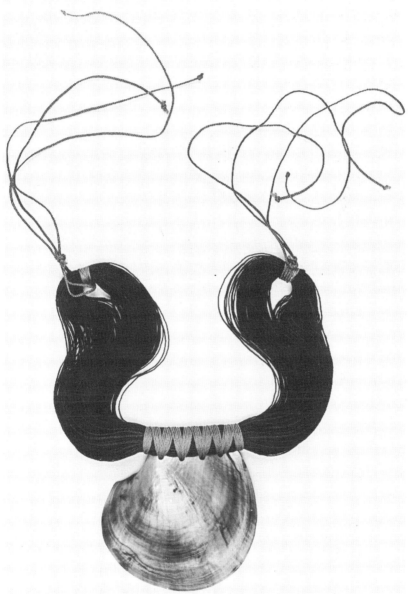

38. Breast ornament; pearlshell suspended on multiple braided cords of human hair; Mangaia. Length of shell 145 mm. (Photograph: British Museum.)

39. Pair of ear pendants; carved ivory from the teeth of a sperm whale, in the form of human testicles. Although the origin of pendants of this type is controversial, this pair was once suspended by cords of human hair from the pierced ears of the wooden image from Rarotonga illustrated in figure 6. Height 28 mm. (George Ortiz Collection. Photograph: British Museum.)

from the teeth of beached sperm whales, and whalebone were shaped into conjoined balls, *rei*, representing human testicles (figure 39) and worn as ear and neck pendants. These were supported, like the pearlshell breast ornaments, on single or multiple strands of finely braided human hair. More elaborate necklets (figure 40) combined the *rei* pendants with other stylised forms: a pig (or dog), a curious 'stepped' shape which may relate to *marae* structures, and a shape which seems to represent a bird's eye view of a chief's stool. The origin of these whale ivory and bone ornaments is controversial. Some authorities believe that the *rei* pendants, and consequently the necklets, originate not on the Cook Islands but in the neighbouring Austral group. Others argue that they are indigenous to the Cook Islands, probably being made on Mangaia or Atiu. The pair of *rei* pendants illustrated here were once attached by cords of human hair to the pierced ears of the Rarotonga figure shown in figure 6. Whether these pendants were made (as the figure certainly was) on Rarotonga itself or acquired through trade or battle from a neighbouring island such as Mangaia, or a further source in the Austral Islands, remains open to question. Archaeological evidence has so far failed to support the assumption that there was regular communication between the Cook Islands and neighbouring island groups, although it would seem surprising if there was none at all.

The art of fashioning birds' feathers into striking and colourful forms of decoration appears to have been of great importance on the Cook Islands. Before European contact the very limited range of other animals — pigs, dogs, rats, bats and a few species

40. Necklet; sennit wrapped with braided human hair (partly missing) and supporting pendants of carved whalebone in the form of human testicles, the tops of chiefs' stools and other symbols of chiefly authority and power. The origin of these necklets, like the pendants in figure 39, is unclear; they may have been made in the Cook Islands or in other islands of East Polynesia such as the Austral group. Length 230 mm. (Photograph: National Museums of Scotland, Ken Smith.)

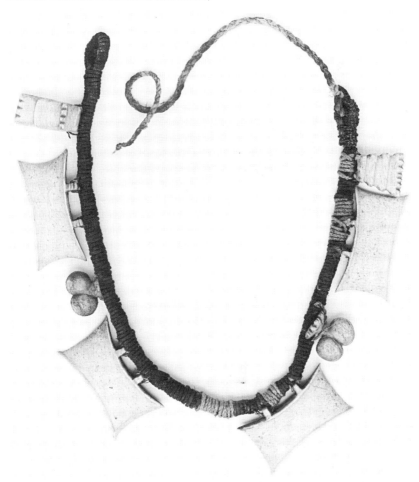

41. Ceremonial head-dress; Atiu. An elaborate construction of black, red and yellow feathers, human hair and white shells supported on a superstructure of thin wooden rods secured with sennit to a conical cap of coiled sennit. Several different techniques are used to secure the feathers. Height 1.020 metres. (Photograph: British Museum.)

of snake — contrasted with the far greater variety of bird species, which, especially in the luxuriant southern islands, included a number bearing spectacular plumage. Unfortunately feathers are a less lasting form of ornament than carved ivory and shell, although even more ephemeral are the widely used fresh scented flowers and leaves so loved by Polynesians. However, a few objects in museums with surviving extensive feather decoration offer a glimpse of the shimmering splendour that once adorned Cook Islands art (figure 41). Red parakeet feathers were highly prized throughout Polynesia, and Captain Cook commented more than once on their significance as an item of trade. The long red tail-feathers of the tropic-bird and black 'man-of-war' hawk feathers were also sought after, together with the feathers of sea-birds and even domestic chickens. On the Cook Islands crescentic necklets covered with feathers and feather ear ornaments were worn. But ceremonial regalia, including head-dresses, caps, headbands and shields, achieved the greatest complexity in construction and design. Feathers were fashioned into streamers, grouped in tufts to form clusters and rosettes with sennit wrapping, or attached to a foundation made of fibre, sennit or wood. The most elaborate feather structures used a wide range of materials, including human hair and painted barkcloth, and must have been prepared for only the most significant occasions. Early European observers remarked on the splendour of Cook Islands feather head-dresses, noting that the islanders considered them to be well worth fighting for.

In contrast to the complex vocabulary of adornment in daily life and on special ceremonial occasions, traditional Cook Islands society used the simplest of clothing. In response to the hot and humid climate men wore only a loin covering and women a short wrap-over skirt. Either sex might add a cloak in cool weather or wear an open-sided poncho (figure 42). The poncho is an unusual garment in Polynesia, recorded only for the Cook and Society Islands and believed to have been in use before contact with Europeans. Islanders went barefoot, although special sandals of plaited hibiscus fibre were worn to protect the feet from sharp coral on the reefs (figure 43). Fresh leaves and leaf fibre were universally used for loin coverings and skirts, but in the southern islands the preferred material for clothing was barkcloth.

The finest barkcloth was made from the inner bark of the paper mulberry plant, although the bark of breadfruit and occasionally banyan trees was also used for coarser grades of cloth. Barkcloth manufacture in the Pacific is a highly skilled, labour-intensive

42. Poncho; a length of stained red-brown barkcloth with a central hole for the wearer's head, decorated with cut perforations to form a pattern, the lower edges slit into a deep fringe; Mangaia. Length 1.280 metres. (Photograph: British Museum.)

process which is generally the work of women. For a thorough survey of the techniques and products of this important and traditional activity in Polynesia, the reader is referred to another book in the Shire Ethnography series, *Polynesian Barkcloth* by Simon Kooijman. The manufacturing process in the Cook Islands was similar to that in other parts of Polynesia, involving preparation of the stripped bast fibre, and beating the strips with wooden beaters on wooden anvils to expand and felt them together until the desired size was achieved. The completed cloth could then be dyed or painted if required (figure 44). Cutwork decoration was also used on barkcloth ponchos in the Cook Islands. Although large quantities of Pacific barkcloth have survived from the nineteenth century, documented examples

43. Reef sandals; braided hibiscus fibre; Atiu. Worn to protect the feet from sharp coral on the reef; made in 1983. Length of sole 230 mm. (Photograph: National Museums of Scotland, Ken Smith.)

from the Cook Islands are relatively rare in museum collections. Barkcloth was used in the Cook Islands for loincloths, belts or girdles, skirts, cloaks and ponchos, and as room dividers and bedding. It had ceremonial as well as secular functions and was often an important component in the ritual 'dress' of religious carvings such as staff gods. An unusual use of barkcloth in the Polynesian context is for masks, which were worn by ceremonial dancers on Mangaia. Peaked, and painted with black designs, these structures of barkcloth supported on a cane frame covered

44. Man's waistband of barkcloth, painted with a black geometric design; Rarotonga. Total length 4.325 metres. (Photograph: National Museums of Scotland, Ken Smith.)

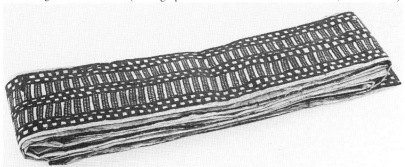

45. Basket; coconut leaf; Atiu. Made by splitting part of a coconut leaf along its midrib and plaiting the leaflets in such a way that the bent midrib forms the rim of the basket, the free ends of the leaflets being tied to close the bottom. Loop handles of braided hibiscus fibre. Made in 1981. Length 685 mm. (Photograph: National Museums of Scotland, Ken Smith.)

the entire head and face of the wearer in the manner of a hood. Their use on Mangaia is recorded in early twentieth-century photographs and they may be a post-European innovation. Very few examples of Cook Islands masks survive in museum collections.

The production of barkcloth for clothing declined quickly on the Cook Islands following contact with Europeans and the subsequent introduction of woven cotton fabric. Initially the missionaries endeavoured to teach the people of Rarotonga to spin and weave cotton themselves, but the hand-crafted cloth they produced under the supervision of Manchester artisans was coarse and inferior to the machine-made coloured calicoes offered by numerous American whaling ships in return for fresh food, and this enterprise was short-lived.

Besides the processing of bark, other plant products were of great importance to Cook Islands material culture. The leaves of the ubiquitous coconut palm were plaited into the large sheets used for house roofs and walls, and for food platters, mats, fans, eye shades and baskets. The preparation and processing of palm and pandanus leaves, the latter generally used for the finer plaited items, was a distinctive art. Baskets and bags were of special importance for all manner of carriage and storage. They could be quickly made on the spot for transporting produce from the field to the house (figure 45), or they might be carefully worked and decorated in order to store a precious personal ornament or a fragile item of ceremonial regalia (figure 46). Fine pandanus mats for bedding and floor coverings had decorative patterns similar to those on the fine bags (figure 47). Plaited fans were widely used, from the simple version with a handle formed by the midrib of the coconut leaf itself, to finely worked wide triangular twilled fans supported on beautifully carved wooden handles which were reserved for individuals of importance (figure

46. Bag; pandanus leaf; Rarotonga. Woven with a geometric pattern in dyed red-brown and black split leaf. Width 480 mm. (Photograph: British Museum.)

47. Mat; pandanus leaf; Rarotonga. Decorated with bands of complex geometric designs in black split pandanus. Length 1.880 metres. (Photograph: British Museum.)

22). Early observers referred to fans of 'outrageous size' which men of the highest status carried, rather in the manner of an umbrella, to ward off sun and rain.

6
Cook Islands art today

Life in the Cook Islands has altered irrevocably since the first contact with Europeans took place in the late eighteenth century. The initial impact of change was brought about by two factors, metal and missionaries.

Aspects of material culture, the things made and worn and used, are often the quickest to respond to change. The introduction of metal technology, chiefly in the form of iron nails, knives and axe-heads, was seized upon by a neolithic people who quickly abandoned their traditional stone implements. The use of the stone adze as the typical tool and of sennit lashing as the typical method of fastening ceased, and today no one on the Cook Islands can make a traditional stone adze-head although there are some who can still process sennit.

The rapid adoption of the Christian faith by a high proportion of the population had a profound effect on local religion and traditional concepts regarding the ordering of society. The elaborate balance of a social structure and belief system focused on deified ancestors foundered, taking with it the basis of traditional authority and law. This too led to material change, since almost at a stroke the carvings of gods and other paraphernalia connected with Cook Islands religion were removed and the *marae* deserted. Before long, copies of enclosed churches imitating Western forms replaced the open-air temples, garments of leaves and barkcloth were replaced by Western-style clothing in Western fabrics and, although the islanders have never lost their love of personal display, the production of traditional ornaments declined. Warfare was drastically reduced and weapons were no longer made. This benefit for the population was, however, outweighed by the enormous loss of life caused by the introduction of European diseases.

Although some aspects of Cook Islands material culture quickly suffered a fundamental blow, others were slower to decline. The manufacture of traditional forms of domestic utensils, bowls, baskets, mats, and the construction of houses and canoes using largely traditional materials continued during the first part of the nineteenth century with only gradual modifications. But, once European and American traders began to exploit the rich resources of the Pacific, whales, turtles, sandalwood and pearls, for Western markets, commercial interests increased.

Traders established business companies on the islands, and new farming methods were introduced altering the ancient economic base of fishing and horticulture. The dramatic developments in global communications brought about in the second half of the nineteenth century by steamships and in the twentieth century by air travel and telecommunications have finally made all the material manifestations of the modern world available to the islands of the Pacific and their inhabitants, and the pressure of change has never been more intense.

Today Avarua, the capital of the Cook Islands on Rarotonga, is a thriving modern community with a busy airport, hotels, shops and restaurants. The copra (dried coconut meat) farmers of Rarotonga drive to their coconut plantations in Japanese-made vans, and copra itself, once the major Cook Islands export, is now being joined by new products, such as cotton quilts and hand-blocked ballet slippers.

Yet on Rarotonga and on other islands in the group the degree of change is far from uniform. The traditional framework of family land-ownership is still acknowledged and, although some of the arts of the Cook Islands such as stoneworking and feather work are lost forever, others, like barkcloth, show signs of revival and wood-carving, basketry and mat-making have persisted, adapting to new demands and evolving new forms. It is remarkable that while the wooden coconut grater with seat is giving way to the electric grater and the hand-carved canoe bailer has been replaced by a cut-down plastic detergent bottle the immense canoe-shaped wooden containers of Atiu are still made, although now used for soaking locally grown coffee beans before husking.

Much artistic activity is now devoted to and determined by the tourist market which is developing rapidly throughout the Pacific. Modern tourists, travelling by air and with a restricted baggage allowance, seek light portable souvenirs tailored to fit a standard suitcase. Shell ornaments and jewellery, small items of wood-carving and basketry, preferably designed to have a use in the purchaser's own environment, are made in considerable quantities for this purpose. Although large foreign industrial manufacturers are already machine-printing barkcloth-style patterns on to factory cotton by the metre for sale at tourist shops in hotels and airports throughout the Pacific, most of these articles are still hand-made on the island of origin.

Through an outlet on Rarotonga, a Cook Islands women's co-operative successfully markets a range of attractive and well made plaited and basketry products, for both tourists and local use. The deft manipulative skills now applied to handbags, hats and place-mats can still reproduce a traditional style of basket (figure 45) or a pair of reef shoes (figure 43) if required. Carvers in the workshop of a family-run craft business in Avarua produce the kind of souvenir, jewellery, ashtrays and small figures, known to appeal to tourists. But they are also able to make exact replicas of the artefacts their ancestors would have made and used. Several of the objects illustrated in this book, including the chief's stool (figure 23), the pounding table (figure 21) and the canoe bailer (figure 28), are contemporary reproductions of traditional forms commissioned for a museum collection. This workshop has also successfully replicated the Rarotongan standing figure (figure 5) and the staff god surmounted by two figures (figure 10). Copied not from the three-dimensional originals but only from drawings and photographs, they testify that the skills, virtuosity and confidence of contemporary Cook Islands carvers are equal to those of the past.

7
Museums

The following are the principal museums with collections of Cook Islands art.

Great Britain

Cambridge University Museum of Archaeology and Anthropology, Downing Street, Cambridge CB2 3DZ. Telephone: 0223 333516 or 337733.

Hunterian Museum, The University of Glasgow, Glasgow G12 8QQ. Telephone: 041-330 4221.

Museum of Mankind (The Ethnography Department of the British Museum), 6 Burlington Gardens, London W1X 2EX. Telephone: 071-323 8043.

Paisley Museum and Art Galleries, High Street, Paisley, Renfrewshire PA1 2BA. Telephone: 041-889 3151.

Pitt Rivers Museum, South Parks Road, Oxford OX1 3PP. Telephone: 0865 270927.

Royal Museum of Scotland, Chambers Street, Edinburgh EH1 1JF. Telephone: 031-225 7534.

Cook Islands

Cook Islands Library and Museum, near Church, Avarua, Rarotonga.

Germany (West)

Staatliches Museum für Volkerkunde, Maximilianstrasse 42, 8000 Munich 22, Bavaria.

Netherlands

Rijksmuseum voor Volkenkunde, Steenstraat 1, 2300 AE, Leiden, Zuid Holland.

New Zealand

Auckland Institute and Museum, The Domain, Auckland 1.

Canterbury Museum, Rolleston Avenue, Christchurch 1, Canterbury Province.

Otago Museum, Great King Street, Dunedin, Otago Province.

United States of America

American Museum of Natural History, 79th Street and Central Park West, New York, NY 10024.

Bernice Pauahi Bishop Museum, 1355 Kalihi Street, Honolulu, Hawaii 96819.

Peabody Museum of Archaeology and Ethnology, 11 Divinity Avenue, Cambridge, Massachusetts 02138.

Peabody Museum of Salem, 161 Essex Street, Salem, Massachusetts 01970.

8
Further reading

Archey, G. *The Art Forms of Polynesia.* Bulletin 4, Auckland Institute and Museum, Auckland, 1965.

Barrow, T. *Art and Life in Polynesia.* Pall Mall Press, London, 1971.

Barrow, T. *The Art of Tahiti and the Neighbouring Society, Austral and Cook Islands.* Thames and Hudson, London, 1979.

Bellwood, P. *The Polynesians: Prehistory of an Island People.* Thames and Hudson, London, 1978.

Buck, P. H. *Ethnology of Manihiki and Rarotonga.* Bulletin 99, B. P. Bishop Museum, Honolulu, 1932.

Buck, P. H. *Arts and Crafts of the Cook Islands.* Bulletin 179, B. P. Bishop Museum, Honolulu, 1944.

Duff, R. *No Sort of Iron: Culture of Cook's Polynesians.* A Cook Bicentenary Exhibition organised by the Art Galleries and Museums Association of New Zealand, Christchurch, 1969.

Idiens, D. 'A Recently Discovered Figure from Rarotonga', *Journal of the Polynesian Society,* 65, 3 (1976), 359-66.

Kaeppler, A.; Newton, D.; and Gathercole, P. *The Art of the Pacific Islands.* National Gallery of Art, Washington (exhibition catalogue), 1979.

Kooijman, S. *Polynesian Barkcloth.* Shire Publications, Princes Risborough, 1988.

Phelps, S. *Art and Artefacts of the Pacific, Africa and the Americas: The James Hooper Collection.* Hutchinson, London, 1976.

Trotter, M. M. (editor). *Prehistory of the Southern Cook Islands.* Bulletin 6, Canterbury Museum, 1974.

Williams, J. *A Narrative of Missionary Enterprises in the South Sea Islands.* Snow, London, 1837.

Index

Page numbers in italic refer to illustrations